TOO MANY SONGS BY TOM LEHRER

TOO MANY SONGS BY TOM LEHRER

with not enough drawings by Ronald Searle

Piano Arrangements by Tom Lehrer and Frank Metis

Pantheon Books, New York

Library of Congress Cataloging in Publication Data

Lehrer, Tom, 1928-
Too many songs by Tom Lehrer.

1. Music, Popular (Songs, etc.)—United States.
I. Searle, Ronald, 1920-   II. Title.
M1630.18.L44T65   81-47201
ISBN 0-394-51957-4   AACR2
ISBN 0-394-74930-8 (pbk.)

Manufactured in the United States of America
First American Edition

CONTENTS

FOREWORD

The songs in this book were written between World Wars II and III, and all but three of them are from the three LPs I recorded during that memorable period in history. Most of them were intended at the time of conception either as takeoffs on various song types of the day, particularly the more sentimental species, or as commentaries on current events, so that I regarded them as fugacious ephemera which by now should have been of artifactual interest only to scholars (although in what field I can't imagine). It is therefore a source of considerable delight to me that publication of this agglomeration should be warranted at all at this late date. Any royalties will naturally be a source of even greater delight.

Three of the songs are not from my three records. Two of them, 'Silent E' and 'L-Y', were written in the early seventies for an American television series called *The Electric Company*, which was produced by the Children's Television Workshop in a desperate attempt to help young children to learn to read. An animated film accompanied each song. The third, 'I Got It From Agnes', is a recently revised version of a song I used to perform in night clubs in the fifties but did not record because it was what was called in those days a 'party song', i.e., a bit naughty. Today, of course, even though the revision made it naughtier, its innocence borders on naïveté.

The musical congeries that follows owes its existence in part to a rather curious event. An intrepid but not entirely rational young British producer named Cameron Mackintosh took it into his head that what had previously been done to every songwriter from Jacques Brel to Stephen Sondheim might be done to me, namely, a stage production embalming my old songs. The result was a revue entitled *Tomfoolery*, which opened in London in 1980 and has since been produced in various other cities throughout the world without any noticeable ill effects. All the songs used in that show are in this book, including certain alternate lyrics which I wrote for the show.

Revisiting these lighthearted and heavy-handed songs (some say it's the other way around) was somewhat like looking at one's own baby pictures: was that me? (Before I began spending so much time in California, I would have said 'Was that I?') I haven't written any songs of this type lately and probably won't be doing so, so this volume may be regarded as a definitive agglutination. (Well-wishers, however, are constantly suggesting hilarious subject matter, such as the Viet Nam war, the gradual destruction of the environment, our recent presidents, etc., so that I have often felt like a resident of Pompeii who has been asked for some humorous comments on lava.) Anyway, what good are laurels if you can't rest on them?

This is my first foreword, so please forgive me if I'm not doing it right. I believe one is supposed to thank people, but I can't think of anyone.

Except you, of course.

April 1981   Tom Lehrer

Part One

From SONGS BY TOM LEHRER

The Irish Ballad

Words and Music by Tom Lehrer

1. A - bout a maid__ I'll sing a song, Sing rick - e - ty - tick - e - ty -
(2. One) morn - ing in__ a fit of pique, Sing rick - e - ty - tick - e - ty -

tin.__ A - bout a maid I'll sing a song Who did - n't have her
tin.__ One morn - ing in__ a fit of pique, She drowned her fa - ther

fam - 'ly long, Not on - ly did__ she do them wrong, She__
in the creek, The wa - ter tast - ed bad for a week, And we

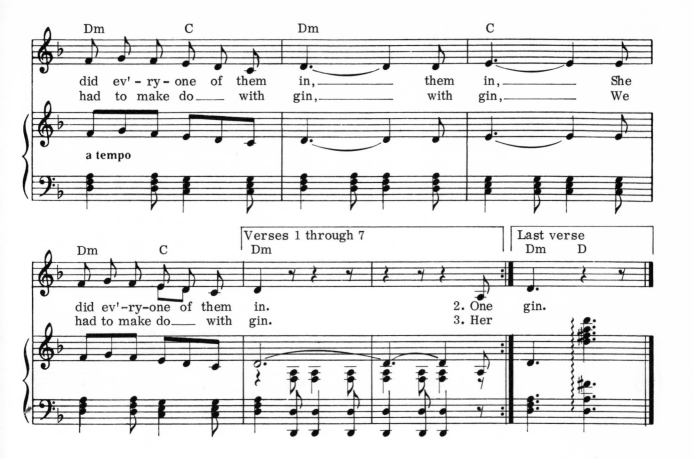

did ev'-ry-one of them in,_____ them in,_____ She
had to make do_____ with gin,_____ with gin,_____ We

Verses 1 through 7
Dm

did ev'-ry-one of them in.
had to make do_____ with gin.

Last verse
Dm   D

2. One   gin.
3. Her

3. Her mother she could never stand,
   Sing rickety-tickety-tin,
   Her mother she could never stand,
   And so a cyanide soup she planned.
   The mother died with the spoon in her hand,
      And her face in a hideous grin, a grin,
      Her face in a hideous grin.

4. She set her sister's hair on fire,
   Sing rickety-tickety-tin,
   She set her sister's hair on fire,
   And as the smoke and flame rose high'r,
   Danced around the funeral pyre,
      Playing a violin, -olin,
      Playing a violin.

5. She weighted her brother down with stones,
   Sing rickety-tickety-tin,
   She weighted her brother down with stones,
   And sent him off to Davy Jones.
   All they ever found were some bones,
      And occasional pieces of skin, of skin,
      Occasional pieces of skin.

6. One day when she had nothing to do,
   Sing rickety-tickety-tin,
   One day when she had nothing to do,
   She cut her baby brother in two,
   And served him up as an Irish stew,
      And invited the neighbors in, -bors in,
      Invited the neighbors in.

7. And when at last the police came by,
   Sing rickety-tickety-tin,
   And when at last the police came by,
   Her little pranks she did not deny,
   To do so, she would have had to lie,
      And lying, she knew, was a sin, a sin,
      Lying, she knew, was a sin.

8. My tragic tale I won't prolong,
   Sing rickety-tickety-tin,
   My tragic tale I won't prolong,
   And if you do not enjoy my song,
   You've yourselves to blame if it's too long,
      You should never have let me begin, begin,
      You should never have let me begin.

Be Prepared

Words and Music by Tom Lehrer

Trustworthily, loyally, helpfully, friendlily, etc.

1. Be pre – pared! _____ That's the Boy Scouts' march-ing song, Be pre-
(2. Be pre –) pared! _____ That's the Boy Scouts' sol-emn creed, Be pre-

pared! _____ As through life you march a – long. Be pre – pared to hold your
pared! _____ And be clean in word and deed. Don't so – lic – it for your

12

li - quor pret - ty well._____ Don't write naugh-ty words on
sis - ter, that's not nice,_____ Un - less you get a good per -

walls if you can't spell._____ Be pre - pared!_____ To hide that
cent-age of her price._____ Be pre - pared!_____ And be

pack of cig - a - rettes, Don't make book_____ if you
care - ful not to do Your good deeds_____ when there's

can not cov - er bets. Keep those reef-ers hid - den where you're sure that
no - one watch-ing you. If you're look-ing for ad - ven - ture of a

they will not be found, And be care-ful not to smoke them when the
new and dif-f'rent kind, And you come a-cross a Girl Scout who is

scout-mas-ter's a-round, For he on-ly will in-sist that they be
si-mi-lar-ly in-clined, Don't be ner-vous, don't be flus-tered, don't be

shared._____ Be pre-pared!
scared._____ Be pre-pared!

2. Be pre-

Fight Fiercely, Harvard!

Words and Music by Tom Lehrer

The Old Dope Peddler

Words and Music by Tom Lehrer

When the shades of night are fall-ing, comes a
eve - ning you will find him, A-

fel - low ev-'ry-one knows. It's the old dope ped - dler, spread-ing
round our neigh - bor - hood. It's the old dope ped - dler do - ing

joy where-ev-er he goes. Ev-'ry good. He
well by do - ing

gives the kids free sam-ples, be-cause he knows full well That to-day's young in-no-cent fa-ces will be to-mor-row's cli-en-tele. Here's a cure for all your trou-bles, here's an end to all dis-tress. It's the old dope ped-dler with his pow-dered hap-pi-ness.

ritard.

The Wild West is Where I Want To Be

Words and Music by Tom Lehrer

A - long the trail you'll find me lop - in' Where the spa - ces are wide
(- 'Mid the) sage - brush and the cac - tus I'll watch the fel - lers

o - pen, In the land of the old A. E.
prac - tice Drop - pin' bombs through the old clean des - ert

C._____ Where the sce-ner-y's at-trac-tive And the
breeze._____ I'll have on my som-bre-ro And of

air is ra-di-o - ac-tive, Oh, the wild west is where I want to
course I'll wear a pair o' Le - vis o - ver my

be._____ 'Mid the lead B. V.

D's. _____ I will leave the cit - y's rush, Leave the

fan - cy and the plush, Leave the snow and leave the slush, And the crowds._____ I will seek the des - ert's hush, Where the sce - ner - y is lush, How I long to see the mush - room clouds._____ 'Mid the

yuc-cas and the this-tles I'll watch the guid-ed mis-siles, While the

old F. B. I. watch-es me. _____ Yes, I'll

soon make my ap-pear-ance (Soon as I can get my clearance),'Cause the

wild west is where I want to be. _____

ritard. e cresc.   *f*

I Wanna Go Back to Dixie

Words and Music by Tom Lehrer

low that Ma - son - Dix - on line. *(Spoken)* Won't - cha

come with me to *Al - a - bam - my, Back to the arms of my dear ol' Mam - my, Her*

*cook - in's lous - y and her hands are clam-my, But what the hell, it's home.(Sung)*Yes, for

Slower

par - a - dise the South-land is my nom-i-nee._____ Jes' give

Lobachevsky

by Tom Lehrer

(Note: Most of the following is meant to be spoken rather than sung, freely in some cases and rhythmically in others. The specific accompaniment used by the author on his recording would require too many pages to write out and is therefore omitted. Prospective performers of the piece are advised to heed its basic precept and plagiarize the author's version.)

(The author would like to state that although Nicolai Ivanovich Lobachevsky (1793-1856) was a genuine, and indeed eminent, mathematician, the peccadillos attributed to him herein are not substantiated by history. The format of this song was suggested by a Danny Kaye—Sylvia Fine routine entitled 'Stanislavsky', and the name of the protagonist was chosen for purely prosodic reasons.)

(Spoken)   Who made me the genius I am today,
The mathematician that others all quote,
Who's the professor that made me that way?
The greatest that ever got chalk on his coat.

(Sung)   One man deserves the credit,
One man deserves the blame,
And Nicolai Ivanovich Lobachevsky is his name.
Hi!
Nicolai Ivanovich Lobach –

(Spoken)   I am never forget the day I first meet the great Lobachevsky.
In one word he told me secret of success in mathematics:
Plagiarize!

Plagiarize,
Let no one else's work evade your eyes,
Remember why the good Lord made your eyes,
So don't shade your eyes,
But plagiarize, plagiarize, plagiarize –
Only be sure always to call it please 'research'.

(Sung)   And ever since I meet this man
My life is not the same,
And Nicolai Ivanovich Lobachevsky is his name.
Hi!
Nicolai Ivanovich Lobach –

(Spoken)   I am never forget the day I am given first original paper
to write.   It was on analytic and algebraic topology of
locally Euclidean metrization of infinitely differentiable
Riemannian manifold.
Bozhe moi!
This I know from nothing.
But I think of great Lobachevsky and get idea – ahah!

(Sung)   I have a friend in Minsk,
Who has a friend in Pinsk,

Whose friend in Omsk
Has friend in Tomsk
With friend in Akmolinsk.
His friend in Alexandrovsk
Has friend in Petropavlovsk,
Whose friend somehow
Is solving now
The problem in Dnepropetrovsk.

And when his work is done -
Haha! - begins the fun.
From Dnepropetrovsk
To Petropavlovsk,
By way of Iliysk,
And Novorossiysk,
To Alexandrovsk to Akmolinsk
To Tomsk to Omsk
To Pinsk to Minsk
To me the news will run,
Yes, to me the news will run!

And then I write
By morning, night,
And afternoon,
And pretty soon
My name in Dnepropetrovsk is cursed,
When he finds out I publish first!

And who made me a big success
And brought me wealth and fame?
Nicolai Ivanovich Lobachevsky is his name.
Hi!
Nicolai Ivanovich Lobach -

(Spoken) I am never forget the day my first book is published.
Every chapter I stole from somewhere else.
Index I copy from old Vladivostok telephone directory.
This book was sensational!
Pravda - well, *Pravda* - *Pravda* said: (**)
It stinks.
But *Izvestia!*   *Izvestia* said: (**)
It stinks.
Metro-Goldwyn-Moskva buys movie rights for six million rubles,
Changing title to 'The Eternal Triangle',
With Ingrid Bergman playing part of hypotenuse.

(Sung)   And who deserves the credit?
And who deserves the blame?
Nicolai Ivanovich Lobachevsky is his name.
Hi!

(**) *At each of these two junctures one should insert some phrase in Russian
(if the audience does not speak Russian) or some Russian double-talk (if it
does). The author's own choices varied from performance to performance,
ranging from the merely inappropriate to the distinctly obscene.*

The Hunting Song

Words and Music by Tom Lehrer

al-ways will re-mem-ber, 'Twas a year a-go No-vem-ber, I went
in no mood to tri-fle, I took down my trust-y ri-fle And went

out to hunt some deer On a morn-ing bright and clear. I went and shot the
out to stalk my prey. What a haul I made that day! I tied them to my

max-i-mum the game laws would al-low, Two game war-dens, sev-en hunt-ers, and a
fen-der and I drove them home some-how, Two game war-dens, sev-en hunt-ers, and a

cow.   I was cow.   The   law was ver-y firm, it

took a-way my per - mit, The worst pun-ish-ment I ev-er en - dured.

It turned out there was a   rea - son,   Cows were out of   sea - son, And

one of the hunt-ers was-n't   in - sured.   Peo-ple   ask me how I

do it, And I say 'There's noth-ing to it, You just stand there look-ing cute, *And when*

some-thing moves, you shoot!' And there's ten stuffed heads in my tro-phy room right

now, Two game war-dens, sev-en hunt-ers and a

pure - bred Guern - sey cow.

I Hold Your Hand in Mine

Words and Music by Tom Lehrer

33

My Home Town

Words and Music by Tom Lehrer

free in my home town. _____ I re-mem-ber
_____ in my home town. _____ I re-mem-ber

Dan, _____ the drug-gist on the cor-ner, 'e was
Sam, _____ he was the vil-lage id-i-ot_____ And

nev-er mean or or-ner-y,___ He was swell._____ He killed his
though it seems a pit-y, it___ was so. _____ He loved to

moth-er-in-law and ground her up real well, And sprin-kled just a bit O-ver
burn___ down hous-es just to watch the glow, And noth-ing could be done 'Cause he

When You Are Old and Gray

Words and Music by Tom Lehrer

Since I still ap-pre-ci-ate you, Let's find love while we may. Be-cause I know I'll hate you, When you are old and gray.

teeth will start to go, dear, Your waist will start to spread. In twen-ty years or so, dear, I'll wish that you were dead.

* The alternative version of the interlude was written for the 1980 revue *Tomfoolery*, *in which it was sung by an older man to a younger man.*

INTERLUDE

aw - ful de - bil - i - ty, A less - ened u - til - i - ty, A
joy-ing our com-pat-i - bil - i - ty, I am cog-ni-zant of its fra - gil - i - ty, And I

loss of mo - bil - i - ty Is a strong pos - si - bil - i - ty. In
question the ad-vis-a - bil - i - ty Of re - ly - ing on its du-ra - bil - i - ty. You're a-

all prob - a - bil - i - ty I'll lose my vi - ril - i - ty And
ware of my in-flex-i - bil - i - ty And my quin-tes-sen-tial vol-a - til-i - ty And the

you your fer - til - i - ty And de - sir - a - bil - i - ty, And
to-tal in-con-ceiv-a - bil - i - ty Of my show-ing gen-u-ine hu - mil-i - ty. Though your

43

The Wiener Schnitzel Waltz

Words and Music by Tom Lehrer

mem-ber the night I held you so tight, As we danced to the
mem-ber the night I held you so tight, As we danced to the

Wie-ner Schnit-zel Waltz._____ The mu-sic was gay and the
Wie-ner Schnit-zel Waltz._____ *(British version:)* *Your lips were like wine (if you'll*
Your face was a - glow (but your

setting was Vi-en-nese, Your hair wore some ro-ses (or per-
par-don the sim-i-le), The mu-sic was love-ly and
teeth rath - er yel-low - ish), The mu - sic was love - ly, quite

haps they were pe-o-nies), I was blind to your ob-vi-ous
quite Ru - dolf Frim-l-y. I drank wine, you drank choc-o-late
I - vor No - vel - lo - ish.

faults, As we danced 'cross the scene to the
malts, And we both turned quite green to the

a tempo

strains of the Wie-ner Schnit-zel Waltz.
strains of the Wie-ner Schnit-zel

Oh, I Waltz.

drank some cham-pagne from your shoe.

I was drunk by the time I got through. For

I did-n't know, as I raised that cup, It had tak-en two

bot-tles to fill the thing up. It was I___ who stepped on your dress_____ The skirts all came off, I con-fess.___ Re - veal-ing for all of the oth-ers to see Just what it was that en-deared you to me.___ Oh, I re-

Part Two

From AN EVENING WASTED
WITH TOM LEHRER

Poisoning Pigeons in the Park

Words and Music by Tom Lehrer

Vernally

Verse

Spring is here, a-suh-puh-ring is here, Life is skit-tles and life is beer, I think the love-li-est time of the year is the spring. *I do, don't you?* Course you

see my sweet-heart and me, As we poi-son the pi-geons in the
do in a squir-rel or two, While we're poi-son-ing pi-geons in the

park. _____ When they see us com-ing, the bird-ies all
park. _____ We'll mur-der them all a-mid laugh-ter and

try an' hide, But they still go for pea-nuts when coat-ed with
mer-ri-ment, Ex - cept for the few we take home to ex -

tempo ad lib.

cy-an-hide. The sun's shin-ing bright, Ev-'ry-thing seems all
per-i-ment. My pulse will be quick-en-in' with each drop of

a tempo

The Masochism Tango

Words and Music by Tom Lehrer

I ache for the touch of your lips, dear, But much more for the touch of your whips, dear. You can raise welts like no-bo-dy else, As we

57

soul is on fire, It's a-flame with de-sire. Which is
Frac-ture my spine, And swear that you're mine, As we

why I per-spire when we tan-go._____ You caught my

dance to the Mas-o - - chis-m Tan-go.

INTERLUDE (somewhat slower)

nose_____ in your left cas-ta - net, love,_____ I can feel the pain
(Alternate:) I can nev-er for -

yet, love, Ev-'ry time I hear drums.
get, love, How this pas - sion was born.

And I en - vy the rose That you held in your
How I en - vied the rose That your teeth used to

teeth, love, With the thorns un - der - neath, love,
clench, love, When I tried some - thing French, love,

Stick-ing in - to your gums. Your
All I got was a thorn.

Somewhat faster (as before)

D.S. al Fine

A Christmas Carol

Words and Music by Tom Lehrer

Christ-mas time is here, by gol - ly,
Dis - ap - pro - val would be fol - ly,
la-tions, spar-ing no expense, 'll Send some use-less old u - ten - sil,

Deck the halls with hunks of hol - ly, Fill the cup and don't say when.
Or a match-ing pen and pen - cil. ('Just the thing I need! How nice!') It

Kill the tur-keys, ducks and chick-ens, Mix the punch, drag out the Dick-ens,
does-n't mat - ter how sin-cere it Is, nor how heart - felt the spir - it,

The Elements

Words by Tom Lehrer
Music by Sir Arthur Sullivan

te - ti - um, va - na - di - um, And lan-tha-num and os-mi-um and as-ta-tine and ra - di - um, And
plat-i-num, plu-to-ni-um, Pal - la-di - um, pro-me-thi-um, po-tas-si-um, po-lo - ni - um, And

gold and pro-tac-ti-ni-um and in-di-um and gal-li-um, And i - o-dine and tho-ri-um and
tan-ta-lum, tech-ne-ti-um, ti - ta-ni-um, tel - lu-ri-um, And cad-mi-um and cal-ci-um and

a tempo

thu - li - um and thal-li - um. There's
chro-mi-um and cu - ri - um. There's

yt-tri-um, yt-ter-bi-um, ac - tin - i - um, rub-id - i - um, And bo-ron, ga-do-lin - i - um, ni-
sul-fur, cal-i-for-ni-um, and fer-mi-um, ber-ke-li-um, And al-so men-de-le-vi-um, ein-

o - bi - um, i - rid - i - um, And stron-ti-um and sil - i-con and sil - ver and sa-ma-ri-um, And
stei-ni-um, no-be-li-um, And ar-gon, kryp-ton, ne-on, ra-don, xe-non, zinc and rho-di-um, And

bis-muth, bro-mine, lith-i - um, be - ryl - li - um, and ba-ri-um.
chlo-rine, car-bon, co-balt, cop-per, tung-sten, tin and so-di - um.

These are the only ones of which the news has come to Ha'vard, And there

poco a poco ritard.

may be man-y oth-ers, but they have-n't been dis-ca-vard.

a tempo

ff

Bright College Days

Words and Music by Tom Lehrer

She's My Girl

Words and Music by Tom Lehrer

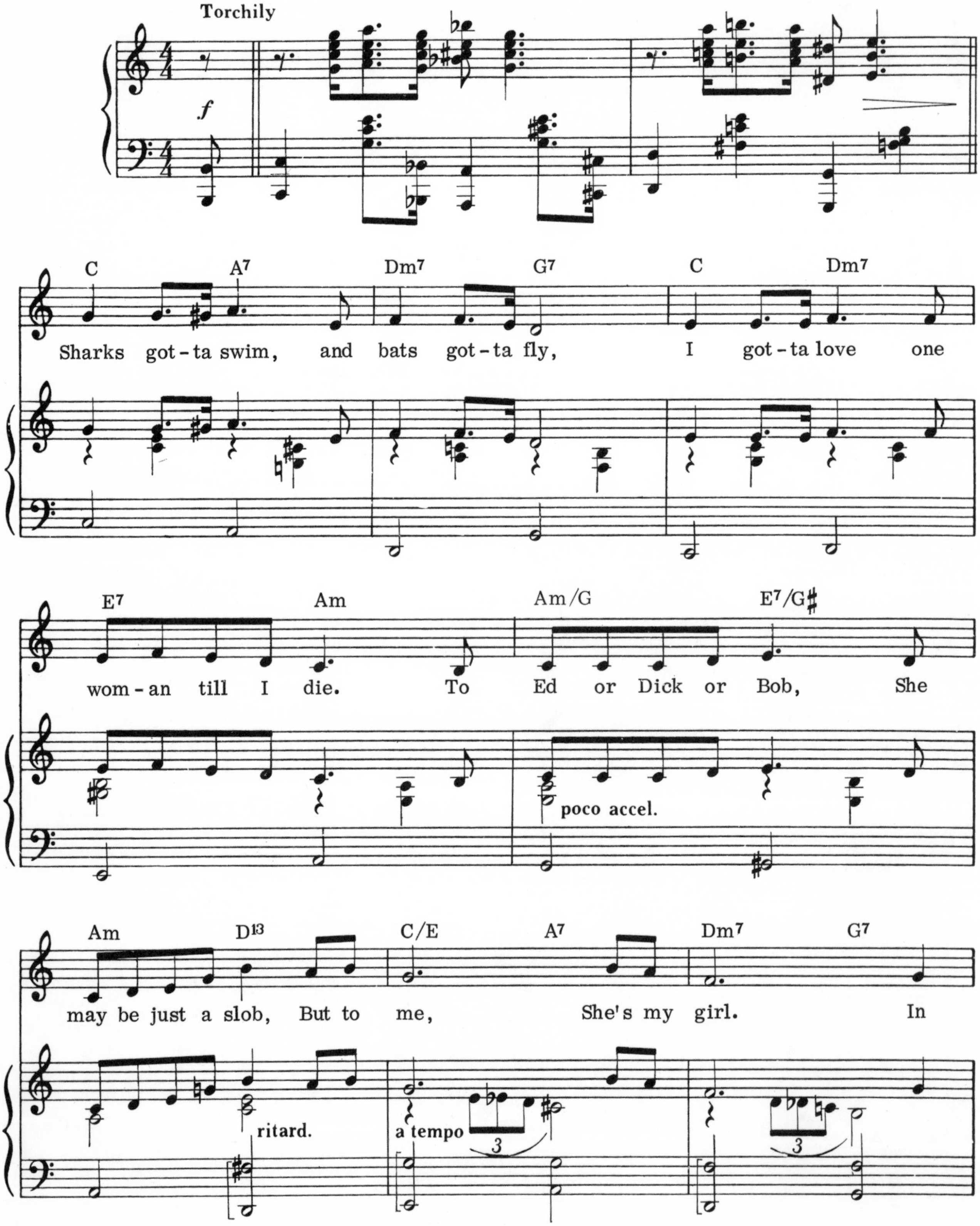

Torchily
f
C A7 Dm7 G7 C Dm7
Sharks got-ta swim, and bats got-ta fly, I got-ta love one
E7 Am Am/G E7/G♯
wom-an till I die. To Ed or Dick or Bob, She
poco accel.
Am D13 C/E A7 Dm7 G7
may be just a slob, But to me, She's my girl. In
ritard.
a tempo
3
3

win-ter___ the bed-room is one large ice cube, And she

squeez-es the tooth-paste from the mid-dle of the tube. Her

hairs in the sink have driv-en me to drink, But she's my

girl, she's my girl, she's my girl, And I

In Old Mexico

Words and Music by Tom Lehrer

When it's fi - es - ta time in Gua - da - la - ja - ra,

Then I long to be back once a - gain In old Mex - i - co.

Where we lived for to-day, nev-er

giv - ing a thought to to - ma - ra_____ To the strum-ming of gui -

tars In a hun-dred grub-by bars I would whis-per 'Te a - mo'._____

The ma - ri - ach - is would ser - e - nade And they

would not shut up till they were paid. We ate, we drank, and we were

mer-ry,   And we got ty-phoid   and dys-en-ter-y.   But

Freely, with motion

best of all,   we   went to the Pla-za de   Tor-os,   Now when-

ev-er I start feel-ing   mo-rose,   I re-vive by re-call-ing that

scene.   And   names_____ like Bel-

mon-te, Do-min-guin, and Ma-no — le - te, If I live to a hun-dred and

eight - e. I shall nev - er for - get what they mean.

Moderately

f **marcato**

gliss.

Fairly fast

(Spoken) For there is surely nothing more beautiful in this world than the sight of a lone man facing
singlehandedly a half a ton of angry pot roast!

f (repeat as necessary)

Out came the mat-a-dor who must have been pot-ted or slight-ly insane, but who looked rath-er bored.

Then the pic-a-dors of course, Each one on his horse. I

shout-ed 'O - lé' ev - 'ry time one was gored.

(Spoken) *Rover was killed by a Pontiac. And it was done with such grace and artistry* The
that the witnesses awarded the driver both ears and tail -- but I digress.

f (repeat as necessary)

mo - ment had come, I swal - lowed my gum, We
crowd held its breath, Hop - ing that death would

knew there'd be blood on the sand pret - ty soon.
bright - en an oth - er - wise dull af - ter - noon.

The At last, the mat - a - dor

poco rit. a tempo

did what we want-ed him to, He raised his sword and his aim was true, In that mo-ment of truth I sud-den-ly knew That some-one had sto-len my wal-let. Now it's fi-es-ta time in Ak-ron, O-hi-o,

freely

a tempo

Moderately

No chord

a tempo

But it's back to old Gua-da-la - ja-ra I'm longing to go.

Far a - way from the strikes of the A. F. of L. and C. I. O.
(Alternate:) For though try, as I may, I can nev - er re-pay all that I owe

How I wish I could get back to the land of the wet-back and for-get the Al - a-
To the land of ma - ña - na And cheap ma-ri - jua-na (It's so ea - sy to

mo, In old Mex-i - co. O - lé!
grow)

cresc. poco a poco

We Will All Go Together When We Go

Words and Music by Tom Lehrer

81

do (but don't you worry.) No more ashes, no more sack- And an armband made of black cloth will
cloth

some-day never more a-dorn a sleeve. For if the bomb that drops on you gets your

friends and neigh-bors too, There'll be no-bod-y left be-hind to grieve.

poco più mosso

Chorus

Moderately bright (in 2)

1. And we will all go to-geth-er when we go,_____
(2. And we will) all bake to-geth-er when we bake,_____

fused   with   an   in - can - des - cent   glow._____   No - one   will
let   there   be   no   moan - ing   of   the   bar._____   Just   sing

have   the   en - du - rance   to   col - lect   on   his   in - su - rance, Lloyd's   of
out   a   Te   De - um   when   you   see   that   I.   C.   B.   M.,   And   the

Lon - don   will   be   load - ed   when   they   go._____   We   will
par - ty   will   be   come-as-you - are._____   We   will

all   fry   to - geth - er   when   we   fry._____   We'll   be
all   burn   to - geth - er   when   we   burn._____   There'll   be

french fried po-ta-toes by and by.___ There will
no need to stand and wait your turn.___ When it's

be no more mis-e-ry when the world is our ro-tis-se-rie, Yes we
time for the fall-out and Saint Pe-ter calls us all___ out, We'll just

all will fry to-geth-er when we fry.___ Down by the
drop our a-gen-das and ad-

old mael - strom,___ There'll be a

storm____ be - fore____ the calm.____ 2. And we will

journ.____ You will all go di-rect-ly to your re-spec-tive Val-

hal - las.____ Go di - rect-ly, do not pass, go, do not col-lect two hun-dred

dol - las.____ And we will all go to - geth - er when we

Part Three

From THAT WAS THE YEAR THAT WAS, etc.

National Brotherhood Week

Words and Music by Tom Lehrer

1. Oh, the white folks hate the black folks, And the black folks hate the white folks. To hate all but the right folks is an old es-tab-lished rule.
2. (Oh, the) poor folks hate the rich folks, And the rich folks hate the poor folks. All of my folks hate all of your folks, it's A - mer-i-can as ap-ple pie.
3. (Oh, the) Prot-es-tants hate the Cath-o-lics, And the Cath-o-lics hate the Prot-es-tants, And the Hin-dus hate the Mos-lems, and ev'-ry-bo-dy hates the Jews.

_____ But dur-ing Na - tion - al Broth-er-hood Week, Na - tion - al
_____ But dur-ing Na - tion - al Broth-er-hood Week, Na - tion - al
_____ But dur-ing Na - tion - al Broth-er-hood Week, Na - tion - al

Last time to Coda

Broth-er-hood Week, Le - na Horne and Sher- iff Clark are danc - ing
Broth-er-hood Week, New York-ers love the Puer-to Ri-cans 'cause it's

cheek to cheek, It's fun to eu - lo - gize___ the peo - ple
ver - y chic, Step up and shake the hand___ of some - one

you de-spise.___ As long as you don't let 'em in your school.
you can't stand,___ You can tol - e - rate him if you try.

2. Oh, the
3. Oh, the

MLF Lullaby

Words and Music by Tom Lehrer

Wiegenliedig

mp

C   G7

Sleep, ba-by, sleep, in peace may you slum-ber, No dan-ger lurks, your
Why should-n't they have nu-cle-ar war-heads? Eng-land says no, but

mp

C   C7   F   Fm   C   G   A7

sleep to en-cum-ber, We've got the mis-siles, peace to de-ter-mine, And
they all are sore-heads, I say a by-gone should be a by-gone,

G7sus4   G7   G7sus4   G7   C

one of the fin-gers on the but-ton will be Ger-man.
Let's make peace the way we did in Stan-ley-ville and Sai-gon.

Once all the Ger – mans were war – like and mean, But that could-n't hap – pen a –

gain. We taught them a les – son in nine – teen eight-een, And

they've hard – ly both-ered us since then. So sleep well, my dar – ling, the
(Alternate:) So sleep, ba – by, sleep, your

poco rit. *a tempo*

The Folk Song Army

Words and Music by Tom Lehrer

Earnestly

We are the Folk Song Ar-my, Ev-'ry-one of us
are in-noc-u-ous folk songs, But we re-gard 'em with
-ray for the Folk Song Ar-my, We will show you the

cares. We all hate pov-er-ty, war, and in-jus-tice, *(Spoken)*
scorn. The folks who sing 'em have no so-cial con-science. Why,
way. 'Cause we all hate po-ver-ty, war and in-jus-tice, And

un-like the rest of you squares. There they don't e-ven care if
(Alternate:) Hoo - chords that are too hard to

Jim - my Crack Corn. (Sung) If you feel dis-sat-is-fac-tion,
play.

ain't good Eng - lish, and it don't e - ven got-ta rhyme._Excuse me - rhyne! Re -

mem - ber the war a - gainst Fran - co?_____ That's the

kind where each of us be - longs,_____ Though

he may have won all the bat - tles,_____ We had

Smut

Words and Music by Tom Lehrer

Smut!
thrill

Give me smut and noth - ing but!
to an - y book like "Fan - ny Hill."

A dir - ty nov - el I can't shut,
And I sup - pose I al - ways will,

if it's un-
if it is

cut,
swill,

and un-subt — — (t)le.
and real-ly fil — — thy.

Por - - - no-graph-ic pic-tures I a - dore,
Smut! Like the ad-ven-tures of a slut,

In-de - cent mag - a-zines ga-lore, I like them
Oh, I'm a mar-ket they can't glut, I don't know

more if they're hard core!

what com-pares with smut, hip hip hoo -

ray! *(Spoken) Let's hear it for the Supreme Court!* Don't *(Sung)* let them take it a - way!

(Spoken) Bring on the obscene movies, murals, postcards, neckties, samplers, stained-glass windows, tattoos, anything! More, more, I'm

still not satisfied!   *(Sung)* Sto - ries of tor - tures, used by de-

bauch - ers, lu - rid, li - cen - tious and vile, Make me

smile.   Nov - els that pan - der to

my taste for can - dor give me a pleas - ure__ sub - lime.__ *(Spoken) Let's*

face it, I love slime. *(Sung)* All books can be in-de-cent books though

re-cent books are bold-er, For filth (I'm glad to say) is in the mind of the be-

hold-er; When cor-rect-ly viewed, ev-'ry-thing is lewd. *(Spoken) I could*

tell you things a-bout Pe-ter Pan, And the Wiz-ard of Oz, there's a dir-ty old man! I *(Sung)*

Send the Marines

Words and Music by Tom Lehrer

When some-one makes a move of which we don't ap - prove, Who is it that
(We'll) send them all we've got, John Wayne and Ran-dolph Scott, Re-mem-ber those ex-

al-ways in - ter-venes? U. N. and O. A. S., They have their place, I
cit-ing fight-ing scenes? To the shores of Trip-o-li, but not to Mis-sis-

guess, But first send the Ma-rines! We'll What do we do?
sip-po-li,

We send the Ma-rines! For might makes right, And

till they've seen the light, they've got to be pro-tect-ed, all their rights re-

spect-ed, Till some-bod-y we like can be e-lect-ed. Mem-bers of the

corps all hate the thought of war, They'd rath-er kill them off by peace-ful means. Stop call-ing it ag-gres-sion, we hate that ex-pres-sion, We on-ly want the world to know that we sup-port the sta-tus quo, They love us ev-'ry-where we go, So when in doubt,____ send the Ma-rines!____

New Math

Words and Music by Tom Lehrer

(Note: Except for the refrain there is no melody to this song. The words are to be spoken rhythmically to an underlying 2/4 beat, except for the words in italics, which are spoken freely. The specific accompaniment used by the author on his recording would require too many pages to write out and is therefore omitted.)

$$\begin{array}{r} 342 \\ -173 \\ \hline 169 \end{array}$$

You can't take three from two,
Two is less than three,
So you look at the four in the tens place.
Now that's really four tens,
So you make it three tens,
Regroup, and you change a ten to ten ones,
And you add them to the two and get twelve,
And you take away three, that's nine.
Is that clear?

Now instead of four in the tens place
You've got three,
'Cause you added one,
That is to say, ten, to the two,
But you can't take seven from three,
So you look in the hundreds place.

From the three you then use one
To make ten tens...
(And you know why four plus minus one
Plus ten is fourteen minus one?
'Cause addition is commutative, right!)...
And so you've got thirteen tens,
And you take away seven,
And that leaves five...

Well, six actually,
But the idea is the important thing!

Now go back to the hundreds place,
And you're left with two,
And you take away one from two,
And that leaves... ?

Everybody get one?
Not bad for the first day!

(Sing refrain)

Now, actually, that is not the answer that I had in mind, because the
book that I got this problem out of wants you to do it in base eight.
But don't panic.   Base eight is just like base ten really – if you're
missing two fingers.   Shall we have a go at it?

$$
\begin{array}{r}
342_{\text{eight}} \\
-173_{\text{eight}} \\
\hline
147_{\text{eight}}
\end{array}
$$

You can't take three from two,
Two is less than three,
So you look at the four in the eights place.
Now that's really four eights,
So you make it three eights,
Regroup, and you change an eight to eight ones,
And you add them to the two,
And you get one-two base eight,
Which is ten base ten,
And you take away three, that's seven.

Now instead of four in the eights place
You've got three.
'Cause you added one,
That is to say, eight, to the two,
But you can't take seven from three,
So you look at the sixty-fours.

Sixty-four?   "How did sixty-four get into it?"
I hear you cry.   Well, sixty-four is eight squared,
don't you see?   (Well, you ask a silly question,
and you get a silly answer.)

From the three you then use one
To make eight eights,
And you add those eights to the three,
And you get one-three base eight,
Or, in other words,
In base ten you have eleven,
And you take away seven,
And seven from eleven is four.
Now go back to the sixty-fours,
And you're left with two,
And you take away one from two,
And that leaves. . . ?

Now, let's not always see the same hands.
One, right!
Whoever got one can stay after class and clean the erasers.

(Sing refrain)   Hooray for new math,
                              New-hoo-hoo math,
                              It won't do you a bit of good to review math.
                              It's so simple,
                              So very simple,
                              That only a child can do it!

Pollution

Words and Music by Tom Lehrer

1. If you vis-it A-mer-i-can cit-y, You will find_it ver-y pret-ty. Just two things of which you must be-ware: Don't drink the water and don't breathe the air. Pol-lu-tion,_ Pol-lu-tion, They got smog and sew-age and mud,

Turn on your tap and get hot and cold run-ning crud.

2. See the hal - i - buts and the stur - geons be - ing wiped out

by de - ter - geons. Fish gotta swim and birds got-ta fly, But they don't last long

tempo ad lib. *a tempo*

if they try. Pol - lu - tion, Pol - lu - tion, You can use the lat - est tooth-

paste, And then rinse your mouth with in-dus-tri-al

waste.

3. Just go out for a breath of air, And
4. Lots of things there that you can drink, But

you'll be read - y for Med-i-care, The cit - y streets are real-ly
stay a-way from the kitch-en sink, *Throw out your break-fast gar-bage, and I've

2nd time: tempo ad lib.

quite a thrill, If the hoods don't get you the mo-nox-ide will. Pol - lu - tion, Pol-
got a hunch that the folks down-stream will drink it for lunch. So go to the

2nd time: a tempo

*Alternative lyrics may be used here to fit the local situation e.g.
for New York: The breakfast garbage they throw out in Troy/They drink at lunch in Perth Amboy.
for San Francisco: The breakfast garbage that you throw into the Bay /They drink at lunch in San José.

lu - tion,— wear a gas mask and a veil,— Then you— can
cit - y— see the cra - zy peo-ple there,— Like lambs to— the

breathe long— as you don't— in - hale.

slaugh-ter,—

They're drink - ing— the wa - ter— and

breath - ing (cough.........) the air.—

So Long, Mom

(A SONG FOR WORLD WAR III)

Words and Music by Tom Lehrer

So long, mom, I'm off to drop the bomb, so
So long, mom, I'm off to drop the bomb, so

don't wait up for me, _____
don't wait up for me, _____ But

But while you swel — ter down there in your shel — ter,
though I may roam, ___ I'll come back to my home, ___ Al -

You can see me___ on your T. V.,___ While
though it may be___ a pile of de-bris.___ Re-

we're at-tack-ing fron-tal-ly, watch Brink-al-ly and Hun-tal-ly, de-
mem - ber, mom-my, I'm off to get a com-mie, so

scri-bing con-tra-pun-tal-ly the cit-ies we have lost. No
send me a sa-la-mi, and try to smile some-how. I'll

need for you___ to miss a min-ute of the ag-o-niz-ing
look for you___ when the war is o-ver, an hour and a

He was might-y proud when World War Three was de-clared, —
He was-n't scared, — no - sir - ree! — And
this is what he said on his
way to Ar - ma - ged - don:

Who's Next?

Words and Music by Tom Lehrer

Disarmingly

First we got the bomb and that was good, 'cause we love peace and moth-er-hood. Then

Rus-sia got the bomb, but that's o - kay, 'cause the bal-ance of pow - er's main -

tained that way. Who's next? Then France got the bomb but

don't you grieve, 'cause they're on our side (I be-lieve).__ Chi-na got the bomb but

have no fears, 'cause they can't wipe us out for at least five years. Who's__ next?

Ja - pan will have its own de-vice, Tran - sis - tor - ized at

half the price.__ South Af - ri - ca__ wants two, that's right: One for the black and one__

for the white. Who's next? E - gypt's gon - na get one too, Just to use on you know who. So Is - ra - el's get - ting tense, wants one in self de-fense. "The Lord's our shep-herd," says the psalm, But just in case we bet-ter get a

Wernher von Braun

Words and Music by Tom Lehrer

Gently

1. Gath-er round while I sing you of Wern-her von Braun, A man whose al - le - giance is
2.   Some have harsh words for this man of re - nown, But some think our at-ti-tude should

ruled by ex - pe-dience,   Call him a   Na - zi, he   won't e - ven frown,
be one of   grat - i-tude, Like the wid-ows and   crip-ples in   old Lon-don town who

"Na - zi, Shma - zi," says Wern-her von Braun. Don't say that he's hyp-o-
owe their large pen-sions to Wern-her von Braun. You too may be a big

crit-i-cal,_____ Say rath - er that he's a-po-lit-i-cal,_____ "Once the
he - ro,_____ once you've learned to count back-wards to ze - ro,_____ "In

rock-ets are up, who cares where they come down? That's not my de-part-ment," says
Ger-man o-der Eng-lish I know how to count down, Und I'm learning Chi-nese," says

Wern-her von Braun.

Wern-her von Braun.

rall.

125

I Got It From Agnes

(from *Tomfoolery*)

Words and Music by Tom Lehrer

Infectiously

I love my friends,_____ And they love me,_____ We're just as close _____ as we can be._____ And just be-cause _____ we real-ly care, What — ev-er we get, we share!

Chorus

1. I   got it from Ag - nes,   She got it from
2. Giles got it from Daph - ne,   She got it from
3. Max   got it from E - dith, Who gets it ev - 'ry
4. I   got it from Ag - nes, or may - be it was

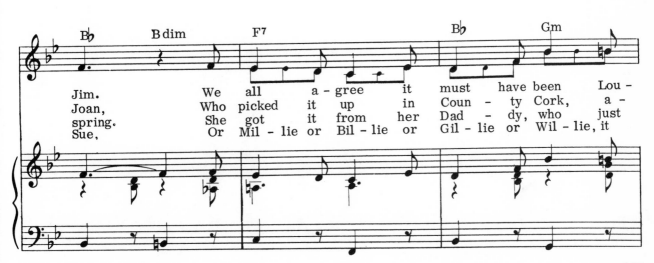

Jim.   We all a - gree it must have been Lou -
Joan,   Who picked it up in Coun - ty Cork, a -
spring.   She got it from her Dad - dy, who just
Sue,   Or Mil - lie or Bil - lie or Gil - lie or Wil - lie, it

ise who gave it to him. Now she got it from
kiss - in' the Blar - ney Stone. Pi - erre gave it to
gives her ev - 'ry - thing. She then gave it to
does - n't mat - ter who. It might have been at the

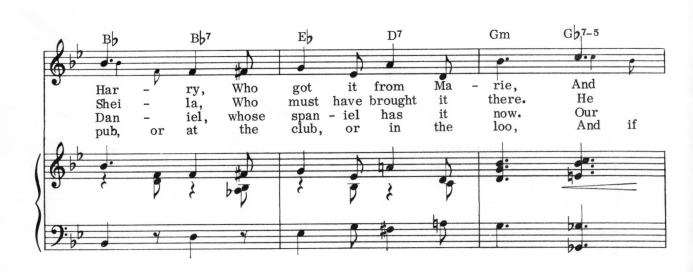

Har - ry, Who got it from Ma - rie, And
Shei - la, Who must have brought it there. He
Dan - iel, whose span - iel has it now. Our
pub, or at the club, or in the loo, And if

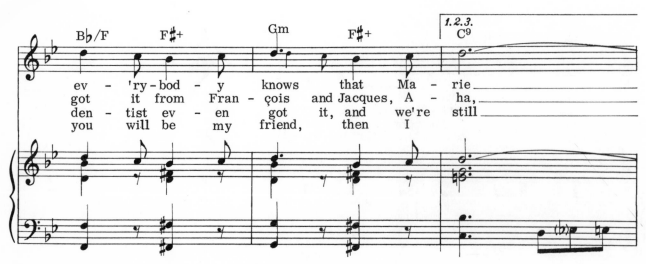

ev - 'ry - bod - y knows that Ma - rie
got it from Fran - çois and Jacques, A - ha,
den - tist ev - en got it, and we're still
you will be my friend, then I

128

got it from me.
Luck-y Pi - erre!
won-der-ing how.

But

might... (Mind you, I said "might")...

cresc. poco a poco

(looks around audience, finally chooses someone, grins, points to him or her and says:)

Give it to you!

f

Silent E

(from *The Electric Company*)

Words and Music by Tom Lehrer

L~Y

(from *The Electric Company*)

Words and Music by Tom Lehrer

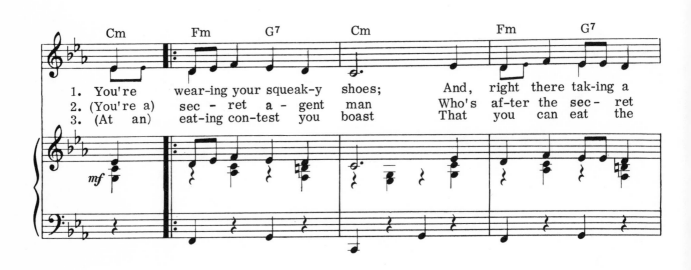

1. You're wear-ing your squeak-y shoes; And, right there tak-ing a
2. (You're a) sec - ret a - gent man Who's af-ter the sec - ret
3. (At an) eat-ing con-test you boast That you can eat the

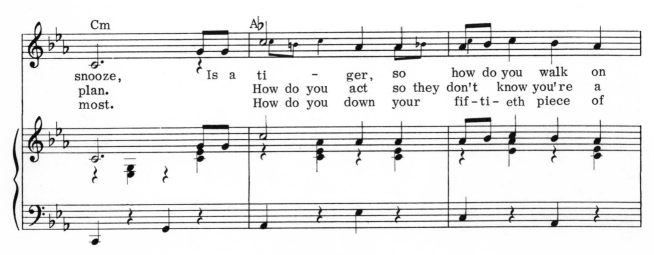

snooze, Is a ti - ger, so how do you walk on
plan. How do you act so they don't know you're a
most. How do you down your fif-ti-eth piece of

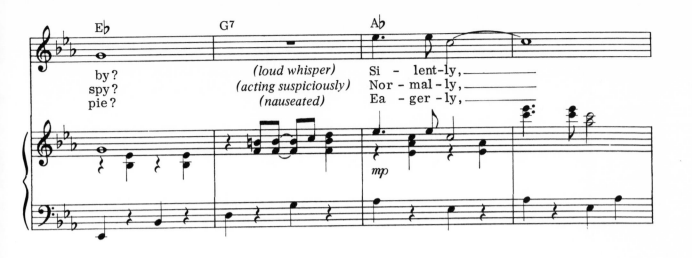

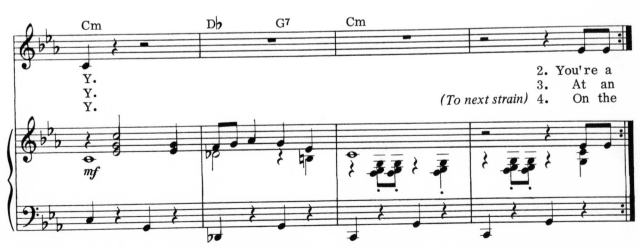

(4.) lake your boat up-set,   And your clothes got soak-ing
5. pub-lic li-bra-ry   You fall and hurt your
6. walk a-long the street   A por-cu-pine you

wet.   How do you stand and wait for them to
knee.   But the sign says QUI - ET PLEASE, so how can you
meet.   How do you shake his hand when he says

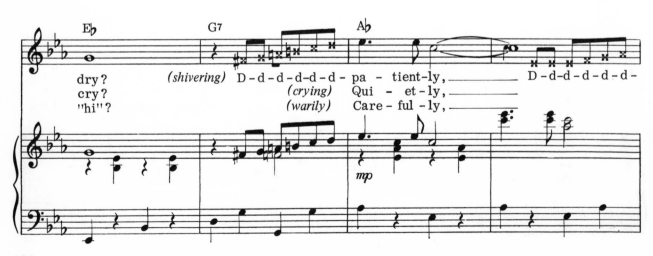

dry?   (shivering) D – d – d – d – d – d – pa – tient-ly,_____ D – d – d – d – d – d –
cry?   (crying) Qui – et-ly,_____
"hi"?   (warily) Care – ful-ly,_____

pa - tient -ly,_____ D - d - d - d - d - d - pa - tient - L.
qui - et - ly,_____ Qui - et - L.
care - ful -ly,_____ Care - ful - L.

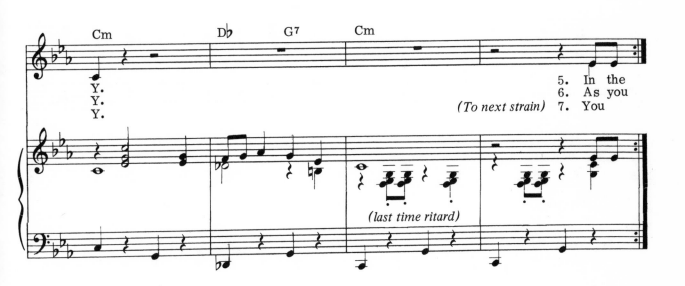

Y.   5. In the
Y.   6. As you
Y.   *(To next strain)* 7. You

(last time ritard)

Slow and sinister (in 2)

en - ter a ver -y dark room, And sit -ting there in the

mf

gloom   Is   Drac - u - la.   Now   how do you say good -

bye?_____   Im - me-di-ate-ly,_____   im -

me-di-ate-ly,_____   Im - me - di - ate - L. -

Y._____   *(Spoken) Bye bye!*

The Vatican Rag

Ecumenically

Words and Music by Tom Lehrer

First you get_ down on your knees,_ Fid-dle with_ your ro-sa-ries,_
So get down_up - on your knees,_ Fid-dle with_your ro-sa-ries,_

Bow your head with great re-spect,_ and gen-u-flect, gen-u-flect, gen-u-flect!
Bow your head with great re-spect,_ and gen-u-flect, gen-u-flect, gen-u-flect!

Do what-ev - er steps you want_if You have cleared them with the Pon-tiff,
Make a cross_on your ab - do - men, When in Rome_do like a Ro - man,

Ev-'ry-bod-y say his own Ky-ri- e e-le- i-son, Do-in' the Vat - i-can
A-ve Ma - ri - a, Gee, it's good to see ya, Get-tin' ec-stat - ic an'

Rag.   sort-a dra-mat - ic an'   do-in' the Vat - i-can

Rag!

Get in line in that pro-ces - sion-al, Step in - to that

140

small con-fes - sion - al, There the guy who's got re - li - gion 'll
tell you if your sin's o - rig - i - nal. If it is___ try
play-in' it sa - fer, Drink the wine and chew the wa - fer,
Two, four, six, eight, Time to tran-sub - stan - ti - ate!

DISCOGRAPHY

(All recordings are LPs unless otherwise noted)

SONGS BY TOM LEHRER
U.S.: Lehrer TL 101 (1953); Reprise RS-6216 (re-recording, 1966)
U.K.: Decca LF 1311 (1958)

Songs: Fight Fiercely, Harvard
The Old Dope Peddler
Be Prepared
The Wild West Is Where I Want to Be
I Wanna Go Back to Dixie
Lobachevsky

The Irish Ballad
The Hunting Song
My Home Town
When You Are Old and Gray
I Hold Your Hand in Mine
The Wiener Schnitzel Waltz

AN EVENING WASTED WITH TOM LEHRER
U.S.: Lehrer TL 202 (1959); Reprise RS-6199 (re-release, 1966)
U.K.: Decca LK 4332 (mono) and SKL 4097 (stereo) (1959)
(Recorded at a concert performance in Cambridge, Massachusetts. A studio recording of the same eleven songs, without the author's spoken comments, was also released in 1959 under the title MORE OF TOM LEHRER (U.S.: Lehrer TL 102; U.K.: Decca LF 1323).)

Songs: Poisoning Pigeons in the Park
Bright College Days
A Christmas Carol
The Elements
Oedipus Rex
In Old Mexico

Clementine
It Makes a Fellow Proud to Be a Soldier
She's My Girl
The Masochism Tango
We Will All Go Together When We Go

TOM LEHRER REVISITED
U.S.: Lehrer TL 201 (1960)
U.K.: Decca LK 4375 (1960)
(A live concert version of the twelve songs from SONGS BY TOM LEHRER. The U.K. version was recorded at a performance in Cambridge, Massachusetts; one side of the U.S. version was taken from the same performance and the other side from some concert performances in Australia.)

POISONING PIGEONS IN THE PARK and THE MASOCHISM TANGO, recorded by the author with an orchestra conducted by Richard Hayman, was released as a single record in 1960 (U.S.: Capricorn C-451; U.K.: Decca 45F-11243).

THAT WAS THE YEAR THAT WAS
U.S.: Reprise RS-6179 (1965)
U.K.: Pye R-6179 (1965)
(Recorded at the hungry i night club in San Francisco.)

Songs: National Brotherhood Week
MLF Lullaby
George Murphy
The Folk Song Army
Smut
Send the Marines
Pollution

So Long, Mom
Whatever Became of Hubert?
New Math
Alma
Who's Next?
Wernher von Braun
The Vatican Rag

SILENT E, recorded by the author with an orchestra conducted by Joe Raposo, appears on THE ELECTRIC COMPANY (U.S.: Warner Brothers BS 2636 (1972), later re-released as Sesame Street CTW 22052).

Note: eighteen of the songs in this book, performed by the four members of the original London cast of the revue TOMFOOLERY, appear on the cast album of that show (U.K.: MMT LP001 (1980)).

INDEX OF SONG TITLES

LYRICS

THE IRISH BALLAD

1. About a maid I'll sing a song,
   Sing rickety-tickety-tin,
   About a maid I'll sing a song
   Who didn't have her fam'ly long.
   Not only did she do them wrong,
   She did ev'ryone of them in, them in,
   She did ev'ryone of them in.

2. One morning in a fit of pique,
   Sing rickety-tickety-tin,
   One morning in a fit of pique,
   She drowned her father in the creek.
   The water tasted bad for a week,
   And we had to make do with gin, with gin,
   We had to make do with gin.

3. Her mother she could never stand,
   Sing rickety-tickety-tin,
   Her mother she could never stand,
   And so a cyanide soup she planned.
   The mother died with the spoon in her hand,
   And her face in a hideous grin, a grin,
   Her face in a hideous grin.

4. She set her sister's hair on fire,
   Sing rickety-tickety-tin,
   She set her sister's hair on fire,
   And as the smoke and flame rose high'r,
   Danced around the funeral pyre,
   Playing a violin, -olin,
   Playing a violin.

5. She weighted her brother down with stones,
   Sing rickety-tickety-tin,
   She weighted her brother down with stones,
   And sent him off to Davy Jones.
   All they ever found were some bones,
   And occasional pieces of skin, of skin,
   Occasional pieces of skin.

6. One day when she had nothing to do,
   Sing rickety-tickety-tin,
   One day when she had nothing to do,
   She cut her baby brother in two,
   And served him up as an Irish stew,
   And invited the neighbors in, -bors in,
   Invited the neighbors in.

7. And when at last the police came by,
   Sing rickety-tickety-tin,
   And when at last the police came by,
   Her little pranks she did not deny.
   To do so she would have had to lie,
   And lying, she knew, was a sin, a sin,
   Lying, she knew, was a sin.

8. My tragic tale I won't prolong,
   Sing rickety-tickety-tin,
   My tragic tale I won't prolong,
   And if you do not enjoy my song,
   You've yourselves to blame if it's too long,
   You should never have let me begin, begin,
   You should never have let me begin.

BE PREPARED

Be prepared! That's the Boy Scouts' marching song,
Be prepared! As through life you march along.
Be prepared to hold your liquor pretty well.
Don't write naughty words on walls if you can't spell.

Be prepared! To hide that pack of cigarettes,
Don't make book if you cannot cover bets.
Keep those reefers hidden where you're sure
    that they will not be found,
And be careful not to smoke them
    when the scoutmaster's around,
For he only will insist that they be shared.
    Be prepared!

Be prepared! That's the Boy Scouts' solemn creed,
Be prepared! And be clean in word and deed.
Don't solicit for your sister, that's not nice,
Unless you get a good percentage of her price.

Be prepared! And be careful not to do
Your good deeds when there's no one watching you.
If you're looking for adventure of a
    new and different kind,
And you come across a Girl Scout who is
    similarly inclined,
Don't be nervous, don't be flustered, don't be scared.
    Be prepared!

FIGHT FIERCELY, HARVARD!

Fight fiercely, Harvard,
    fight, fight, fight!
Demonstrate to them our skill.
Albeit *they* possess the might,
Nonetheless *we* have the will.
How we shall celebrate our victory,
We shall invite the whole team up for tea
    (How jolly!)
Hurl that spheroid down the field, and
Fight, fight, fight!

Fight fiercely, Harvard,
    fight, fight, fight!
Impress them with our prowess, *do!*
Oh, fellows, do not let the crimson down,
Be of stout heart and true.
Come on, chaps, fight for Harvard's glorious name,
Won't it be peachy if we win the game?
    (Oh, goody!)
Let's try not to injure them, but
Fight, fight, fight!
Let's not be rough, though!
Fight, fight, fight!
And do fight fiercely!
Fight, fight, fight!

THE OLD DOPE PEDDLER

When the shades of night are falling,
Comes a fellow ev'ryone knows.
It's the old dope peddler,
Spreading joy wherever he goes.
Ev'ry evening you will find him,
Around our neighborhood.
It's the old dope peddler
Doing well by doing good.

He gives the kids free samples,
Because he knows full well
That today's young innocent faces
Will be tomorrow's clientele.
Here's a cure for all your troubles,
Here's an end to all distress.
It's the old dope peddler
With his powdered happiness.

THE WILD WEST IS WHERE I WANT TO BE

Along the trail you'll find me lopin'
Where the spaces are wide open,
In the land of the old A. E. C.

Where the scenery's attractive,
And the air is radioactive,
Oh, the wild west is where I want to be.

'Mid the sagebrush and the cactus
I'll watch the fellers practice
Droppin' bombs through the clean desert breeze.
I'll have on my sombrero,
And of course I'll wear a pair o'
Levis over my lead B. V. D.'s.

I will leave the city's rush,
Leave the fancy and the plush,
Leave the snow and leave the slush
And the crowds.

I will seek the desert's hush,
Where the scenery is lush,
How I long to see the mush-
     room clouds.

'Mid the yuccas and the thistles
I'll watch the guided missiles,
While the old F. B. I. watches me.
Yes, I'll soon make my appearance
(Soon as I can get my clearance),
'Cause the wild west is where I want to be.

I WANNA GO BACK TO DIXIE

I wanna go back to Dixie,
Take me back to dear ol' Dixie,
That's the only li'l ol' place for li'l ol' me.
Ol' times there are not forgotten,
Whuppin' slaves and sellin' cotton,
And waitin' for the *Robert E. Lee.*
(It was never there on time.)
I'll go back to the Swanee,
Where pellagra makes you scrawny,
And the honeysuckle clutters up the vine.
I really am a-fixin'
To go home and start a-mixin'
Down below that Mason-Dixon line.

Won'tcha come with me to Alabammy,
Back to the arms of my dear ol' Mammy,
Her cookin's lousy and her hands are clammy,
But what the hell, it's home.

Yes, for paradise the Southland is my nominee.
Jes' give me a ham hock and a grit of hominy.

I wanna go back to Dixie,
I wanna be a Dixie pixie
And eat corn pone till it's comin' out of my ears.
I wanna talk with Southern gentlemen
And put my white sheet on again,
I ain't seen one good lynchin' in years.
The land of the boll weevil,
Where the laws are medieval,
Is callin' me to come and nevermore roam.
I wanna go back to the Southland,
That "y'all" and "shet-ma-mouth" land,
Be it ever so decadent,
There's no place like home.

THE HUNTING SONG

I always will remember,
'Twas a year ago November,
I went out to hunt some deer
On a morning bright and clear.
I went and shot the maximum the game laws would
     allow,
Two game wardens, seven hunters, and a cow.

I was in no mood to trifle,
I took down my trusty rifle
And went out to stalk my prey.
What a haul I made that day.
I tied them to my fender, and I drove them home
     somehow,
Two game wardens, seven hunters, and a cow.

The law was very firm, it
Took away my permit,
The worst punishment I ever endured.
It turned out there was a reason,
Cows were out of season,
And one of the hunters wasn't insured.

People ask me how I do it,
And I say "There's nothing to it,
You just stand there looking cute,
And when something moves, you shoot!"
And there's ten stuffed heads in my trophy room right
     now,
Two game wardens, seven hunters, and a pure-bred
     Guernsey cow.

I HOLD YOUR HAND IN MINE

I hold your hand in mine, dear,
I press it to my lips.
I take a healthy bite
From your dainty fingertips.

My joy would be complete, dear,
If you were only here,
But still I keep your hand
As a precious souvenir.

The night you died I cut it off,
I really don't know why.
For now each time I kiss it
I get bloodstains on my tie.

I'm sorry now I killed you,
For our love was something fine,
And till they come to get me
I shall hold your hand in mine.

MY HOME TOWN

I really have a yen
To go back once again,
Back to the place where no one wears a frown,
To see once more those super-special just plain folks
In my home town.

No fellow could ignore
The little girl next door,
She sure looked sweet in her first evening gown.
Now there's a charge for what she used to give for
    free
In my home town.

I remember Dan, the druggist on the corner, 'e
Was never mean or ornery,
He was swell.
He killed his mother-in-law and ground her up real
    well,
And sprinkled just a bit
Over each banana split.

The guy that taught us math,
Who never took a bath,

Acquired a certain measure of renown,
And after school he sold the most amazing pictures
In my home town.

That fellow was no fool
Who taught our Sunday School,
And neither was our kindly Parson Brown.
(Hum)
In my home town.

I remember Sam, he was the village idiot,
And though it seems a pity, it
Was so.
He loved to burn down houses just to watch the glow,
And nothing could be done,
'Cause he was the mayor's son.

The guy that took a knife
And monogrammed his wife,
Then dropped her in the pond and watched her drown.
Oh, yes indeed, the people there are just plain folks
In my home town.

WHEN YOU ARE OLD AND GRAY

Since I still appreciate you,
Let's find love while we may.
Because I know I'll hate you
When you are old and gray.

So say you love me here and now,
I'll make the most of that.
Say you love and trust me,
For I know you'll disgust me
When you're old and getting fat.

*An awful debility,
A lessened utility,
A loss of mobility
Is a strong possibility.
In all probability
I'll lose my virility
And you your fertility
And desirability,
And this liability
Of total sterility

Will lead to hostility
And a sense of futility,
So let's act with agility
While we still have facility,
For we'll soon reach senility
And lose the ability.

Your teeth will start to go, dear,
Your waist will start to spread.
In twenty years or so, dear,
I'll wish that you were dead.

I'll never love you then at all
The way I do today.
So please remember,
When I leave in December,
I told you so in May.

(Alternate:)
While enjoying our compatibility,
I am cognizant of its fragility,
And I question the advisability
Of relying on its durability.
You're aware of my inflexibility
And my quintessential volatility
And the total inconceivability
Of my showing genuine humility.
Though your undeniable nubility
May excuse a certain puerility,
Your alleged indispensability
Underestimates my versatility,
And your boyish irresponsibility
And what now is charming juvenility
Will in time lose their adorability
And appear much more like imbecility.

THE WIENER SCHNITZEL WALTZ

Do you remember the night I held you so tight,
As we danced to the Wiener Schnitzel Waltz?
The music was gay, and the setting was Viennese,
Your hair wore some roses (or perhaps they were
    peonies),
I was blind to your obvious faults,
As we danced 'cross the scene
To the strains of the Wiener Schnitzel Waltz.

Oh, I drank some champagne from your shoe.
I was drunk by the time I got through.
I didn't know as I raised that cup,
For it had taken two bottles to fill the thing up.

It was I who stepped on your dress.
The skirts all came off, I confess.

Revealing for all of the others to see
Just what it was that endeared you to me.

Oh, I remember the night I held you so tight,
As we danced to the Wiener Schnitzel Waltz.
*Your lips were like wine (if you'll pardon the simile),
The music was lovely and quite Rudolf Frimly.
I drank wine, you drank chocolate malts,
And we both turned quite green
To the strains of the Wiener Schnitzel Waltz.

(Alternate:)
Your face was aglow (but your teeth rather yellowish),
The music was lovely, quite Ivor Novello-ish.

POISONING PIGEONS IN THE PARK

Spring is here, a-suh-puh-ring is here.
Life is skittles and life is beer.
I think the loveliest time of the year is the spring.
I do, don't you? "Course you do."
But there's one thing that makes spring complete
    for me,
And makes ev'ry Sunday a treat for me.

All the world seems in tune
On a spring afternoon,
When we're poisoning pigeons in the park.
Ev'ry Sunday you'll see

My sweetheart and me,
As we poison the pigeons in the park.

When they see us coming, the birdies all try an' hide,
But they still go for peanuts when coated with
    cyanide.
The sun's shining bright,
Ev'rything seems all right,
When we're poisoning pigeons in the park.

We've gained notoriety,
And caused much anxiety

In the Audubon Society
With our games.
They call it impiety,
And lack of propriety,
And quite a variety
Of unpleasant names.
But it's not against any religion
To want to dispose of a pigeon.

So if Sunday you're free,
Why don't you come with me,
And we'll poison the pigeons in the park.

And maybe we'll do
In a squirrel or two,
While we're poisoning pigeons in the park.

We'll murder them all amid laughter and merriment,
Except for the few we take home to experiment.
My pulse will be quickenin'
With each drop of strych'nine
We feed to a pigeon.
(It just takes a smidgin!)
To poison a pigeon in the park.

THE MASOCHISM TANGO

I ache for the touch of your lips, dear,
But much more for the touch of your whips, dear.
You can raise welts
Like nobody else,
As we dance to the Masochism Tango.

Let our love be a flame, not an ember,
Say it's me that you want to dismember.
Blacken my eye,
Set fire to my tie,
As we dance to the Masochism Tango.

At your command before you here I stand,
My heart is in my hand. *Ecch!*
It's here that I must be.
My heart entreats,
Just hear those savage beats,
And go put on your cleats and come and trample me.
Your heart's hard as stone or mahogany,
That's why I'm in such exquisite agony.

My soul is on fire,
It's aflame with desire,
Which is why I perspire
    when we tango.

You caught my nose
In your left castanet, love,
*I can feel the pain yet, love,
Ev'ry time I hear drums.
And I envy the rose
That you held in your teeth, love,

With the thorns underneath, love,
Sticking into your gums.

Your eyes cast a spell that bewitches.
The last time I needed twenty stitches
To sew up the gash
You made with your lash,
As we danced to the Masochism Tango.

Bash in my brain,
And make me scream with pain,
Then kick me once again,
And say we'll never part.
I know too well
I'm underneath your spell,
So, darling, if you smell
Something burning, it's my heart.
Excuse me!

Take your cigarette from its holder,
And burn your initials in my shoulder.
Fracture my spine,
And swear that you're mine,
As we dance to the Masochism Tango.

* *(Alternate:)*
I can never forget, love,
How this passion was born.
How I envied the rose
That your teeth used to clench, love,
When I tried something French, love,
All I got was a thorn.

A CHRISTMAS CAROL

Christmas time is here, by golly,
Disapproval would be folly,

Deck the halls with hunks of holly,
Fill the cup and don't say when.

Kill the turkeys, ducks and chickens,
Mix the punch, drag out the Dickens,
Even though the prospect sickens,
Brother, here we go again.

On Christmas Day you can't get sore,
Your fellow man you must adore,
There's time to rob him all the more
The other three hundred and sixty-four.

Relations, sparing no expense, 'll
Send some useless old utensil,
Or a matching pen and pencil.
("Just the thing I need! How nice!")
It doesn't matter how sincere it

Is, nor how heartfelt the spirit,
Sentiment will not endear it,
What's important is the price.

Hark, the *Herald Tribune* sings,
Advertising wondrous things.
God rest you merry, merchants,
May you make the Yuletide pay.
Angels we have heard on high
Tell us to go out and buy!

So let the raucous sleighbells jingle,
Hail our dear old friend Kriss Kringle,
Driving his reindeer across the sky.
Don't stand underneath when they fly by.

THE ELEMENTS

There's antimony, arsenic, aluminum, selenium,
And hydrogen and oxygen and nitrogen and rhenium,
And nickel, neodymium, neptunium, germanium,
And iron, americium, ruthenium, uranium,
Europium, zirconium, lutetium, vanadium,
And lanthanum and osmium and astatine and radium,
And gold and protactinium and indium and gallium,
And iodine and thorium and thulium and thallium.

There's yttrium, ytterbium, actinium, rubidium,
And boron, gadolinium, niobium, iridium,
And strontium and silicon and silver and samarium,
And bismuth, bromine, lithium, beryllium, and
     barium.

There's holmium and helium and hafnium and
     erbium,
And phosphorus and francium and fluorine and
     terbium,

And manganese and mercury, molybdenum,
     magnesium,
Dysprosium and scandium and cerium and cesium.
And lead, praseodymium, and platinum, plutonium,
Palladium, promethium, potassium, polonium,
And tantalum, technetium, titanium, tellurium,
And cadmium and calcium and chromium and curium.

There's sulfur, californium, and fermium, berkelium,
And also mendelevium, einsteinium, nobelium,
And argon, krypton, neon, radon, xenon, zinc, and
     rhodium,
And chlorine, carbon, cobalt, copper, tungsten, tin,
     and sodium.

These are the only ones of which the news has come
     to Ha'vard,
And there may be many others, but they haven't been
     discavard.

BRIGHT COLLEGE DAYS

Bright College Days, Oh, carefree days that fly,
To thee we sing with our glasses raised on high.
Let's drink a toast as each of us recalls
Ivy-covered professors in ivy-covered halls.

Turn on the spigot,
Pour the beer and swig it,
And gaudeamus igit—ur.

Soon we'll be out amid the cold world's strife.
Soon we'll be sliding down the razor blade of life.
But as we go our sordid sep'rate ways,
We shall ne'er forget thee, thou golden college days.

Hearts full of youth,
Hearts full of truth,
Six parts gin to one part vermouth.

SHE'S MY GIRL

Sharks gotta swim, and bats gotta fly,
I gotta love one woman till I die.
To Ed or Dick or Bob
She may be just a slob,
But to me,
She's my girl.

In winter the bedroom is one large ice cube,
And she squeezes the toothpaste from the middle of
   the tube.
Her hairs in the sink
Have driven me to drink,
But she's my girl, she's my girl, she's my girl,
And I love her.

The girl that I lament for,
The girl my money's spent for,
The girl my back is bent for,
The girl I owe the rent for,
The girl I gave up Lent for
Is the girl that heaven meant for me.

So though for breakfast she makes coffee that
   tastes like shampoo,
I come home to dinner and get peanut butter stew,
Or if I'm in luck,
It's broiled hockey puck,
But oh, well, what the hell,
She's my girl,
And I love her.

IN OLD MEXICO

When it's fiesta time in Guadalajara,
Then I long to be back once again
In Old Mexico.
Where we lived for today,
   never giving a thought to tomara.
To the strumming of guitars
In a hundred grubby bars
I would whisper "Te amo."

The mariachis would serenade,
And they would not shut up till they were paid.
We ate, we drank, and we were merry,
And we got typhoid and dysentery.

But best of all, we went to the Plaza de Toros,
Now whenever I start feeling morose,
I revive by recalling that scene.
And names like Belmonte, Dominguín, and
   Manolete,
If I live to a hundred and eight,
I shall never forget what they mean.

*For there is surely nothing more beautiful in this
world than the sight of a lone man facing
   singlehandedly
a half a ton of angry pot roast!*

Out came the matador
Who must have been potted or
Slightly insane, but who looked rather bored.
Then the picadors of course,
Each one on his horse.
I shouted "Olé" ev'ry time one was gored.

I cheered at the banderilleros' display,
As they stuck the bull in their own clever way,
For I hadn't had so much fun since the day
My brother's dog Rover
Got run over.

*Rover was killed by a Pontiac. And it was done with
such grace and artistry that the witnesses awarded the
driver both ears and the tail—but I digress.*

The moment had come,
I swallowed my gum,
We knew there'd be blood on the sand pretty soon.
The crowd held its breath,
Hoping that death
Would brighten an otherwise dull afternoon.

At last, the matador did what we wanted him to,
He raised his sword and his aim was true,
In that moment of truth I suddenly knew
That someone had stolen my wallet.

Now it's fiesta time in Akron, Ohio,
But it's back to old Guadalajara I'm longing to go.
*Far away from the strikes of the A.F. of L. and C.I.O.
How I wish I could get back
To the land of the wetback
And forget the Alamo,
In Old Mexico. Olé!

* (Alternate:)
*For though try, as I may, I can never repay
   all that I owe
To the land of mañana
And cheap marijuana. (It's so easy to grow.)*

WE WILL ALL GO TOGETHER WHEN WE GO

When you attend a funeral,
It is sad to think that sooner o' later
Those you love will do the same for you.
And you may have thought it tragic,
Not to mention other adjectives,
To think of all the weeping they will do.
(But don't you worry.)
No more ashes, no more sackcloth,
And an armband made of black cloth
Will someday nevermore adorn a sleeve.
For if the bomb that drops on you
Gets your friends and neighbors too,
There'll be nobody left behind to grieve.

And we will all go together when we go,
What a comforting fact that is to know.
Universal bereavement,
An inspiring achievement,
Yes, we all will go together when we go.

We will all go together when we go.
All suffused with an incandescent glow.
No one will have the endurance
To collect on his insurance,
Lloyd's of London will be loaded when they go.

We will all fry together when we fry.
We'll be french fried potatoes bye and bye.
There will be no more misery
When the world is our rotisserie,
Yes, we all will fry together when we fry.

Down by the old maelstrom,
There'll be a storm before the calm.

And we will all bake together when we bake,
There'll be nobody present at the wake.
With complete participation
In that grand incineration,
Nearly three billion hunks of well-done steak.

We will all char together when we char,
And let there be no moaning of the bar.
Just sing out a Te Deum
When you see that I. C. B. M.,
And the party will be "come-as-you-are."

We will all burn together when we burn.
There'll be no need to stand and wait your turn.
When it's time for the fallout
And Saint Peter calls us all out,
We'll just drop our agendas and adjourn.

You will all go directly to your respective Valhallas.
Go directly, do not pass Go, do not collect two
    hundred dolla's.

And we will all go together when we go,
Ev'ry Hottentot and ev'ry Eskimo.
When the air becomes uranious,
We will all go simultaneous,
Yes, we all will go together
When we all go together,
Yes, we all will go together when we go.

NATIONAL BROTHERHOOD WEEK

1. Oh, the white folks hate the black folks,
    And the black folks hate the white folks.
    To hate all but the right folks
        Is an old established rule.

    But during National Brotherhood Week,
        National Brotherhood Week,
    Lena Horne and Sheriff Clark are dancing
        cheek to cheek,
    It's fun to eulogize
    The people you despise,
    As long as you don't let 'em in your school.

2. Oh, the poor folks hate the rich folks,
    And the rich folks hate the poor folks.
    All of my folks hate all of your folks,
        It's American as apple pie.

    But during National Brotherhood Week,
        National Brotherhood Week,
    New Yorkers love the Puerto Ricans 'cause
        it's very chic,
    Step up and shake the hand
    Of someone you can't stand,
    You can tolerate him if you try.

3. Oh, the Protestants hate the Catholics,
   And the Catholics hate the Protestants,
   And the Hindus hate the Moslems,
   And ev'rybody hates the Jews.

   But during National Brotherhood Week,
   National Brotherhood Week,

It's National Ev'ryone-smile-at-
   one-another-hood Week,
Be nice to people who
Are inferior to you.
It's only for a week, so have no fear,
Be grateful that it doesn't last all year.

WERNHER VON BRAUN

Gather round while I sing you of Wernher von Braun,
A man whose allegiance
Is ruled by expedience,
Call him a Nazi, he won't even frown,
"Nazi, Shmazi," says Wernher von Braun.

Don't say that he's hypocritical,
Say rather that he's apolitical.

"Once the rockets are up, who cares where they
   come down?
That's not my department," says Wernher von Braun.

Some have harsh words for this man of renown,
But some think our attitude
Should be one of gratitude,
Like the widows and cripples in old London town
Who owe their large pensions to Wernher von Braun.

You too may be a big hero,
Once you've learned to count backwards to zero.
"In German oder English I know how to count down,
Und I'm learning Chinese," says Wernher von Braun.

MLF LULLABY

Sleep, baby, sleep, in peace may you slumber,
No danger lurks, your sleep to encumber,
We've got the missiles, peace to determine,
And one of the fingers on the button will be German.

Why shouldn't they have nuclear warheads?
England says no, but they all are soreheads.
I say a bygone should be a bygone,
Let's make peace the way we did in
      Stanleyville and Saigon.

Once all the Germans were warlike and mean,
But that couldn't happen again.

We taught them a lesson in nineteen eighteen,
And they've hardly bothered us since then.

*So sleep well, my darling, the sandman can linger,
We know our buddies won't give us the finger,
Heil—hail—the Wehrmacht, I mean the Bundeswehr,
Hail to our loyal ally!
MLF
Will scare Brezhnev,
I hope he is half as scared as I.

* (Alternate:)
*So sleep, baby, sleep, your eyes should be shuttin',
We know our buddies won't fool with the button.*

THE FOLK SONG ARMY

We are the Folk Song Army,
Ev'ryone of us cares.
We all hate poverty, war, and injustice,
Unlike the rest of you squares.

*There are innocuous folk songs,
But we regard 'em with scorn.

The folks who sing 'em have no social conscience.
Why, they don't even care if Jimmy Crack Corn.

If you feel dissatisfaction,
Strum your frustrations away,
Some people may prefer action,
But give me a folk song any old day.

The tune don't have to be clever,
And it don't matter if you put a coupla extra
    syllables into a line.
It sounds more ethnic if it ain't good English,
And it don't even gotta rhyme—excuse me—rhyne.

Remember the war against Franco?
That's the kind where each of us belongs.
Though he may have won all the battles,
We had all the good songs.

So join in the Folk Song Army,
Guitars are the weapons we bring
To the fight against poverty, war, and injustice.
Ready! Aim! Sing!

* *(Alternate:)*
Hooray for the Folk Song Army,
We will show you the way.
'Cause we all hate poverty, war, and injustice,
And chords that are too hard to play.

SMUT

Smut!
Give me smut and nothing but!
A dirty novel I can't shut,
If it's uncut,
and unsubt——le.

I've never quibbled
If it was ribald,
I would devour where others merely nibbled.
As the judge remarked the day that he
    acquitted my Aunt Hortense,
"To be smut
It must be ut-
Terly without redeeming social importance."

Por-
Nographic pictures I adore,
Indecent magazines galore,
I like them more
If they're hard-core!

Bring on the obscene movies, murals, postcards,
    neckties,
samplers, stained-glass windows, tattoos, anything!
More, more, I'm still not satisfied!

Stories of tortures
Used by debauchers,
Lurid, licentious, and vile,
Make me smile.
Novels that pander
To my taste for candor
Give me a pleasure sublime.
Let's face it, I love slime.

All books can be indecent books
Though recent books are bolder,
For filth (I'm glad to say) is in the mind
    of the beholder.
When correctly viewed,
Ev'rything is lewd.
I could tell you things about Peter Pan,
And the Wizard of Oz, there's a dirty old man!

I thrill
To any book like *Fanny Hill*,
And I suppose I always will,
If it is swill
And really fil——thy.

Who needs a hobby like tennis or philately?
I've got a hobby: rereading *Lady Chatterley*.
*But now they're trying to take it all away from us
    unless
We take a stand, and hand in hand we fight for
    freedom of the press,
In other words,
Smut!
Like the adventures of a slut.
Oh, I'm a market they can't glut,
I don't know what
Compares with smut.
Hip hip hooray!
Let's hear it for the Supreme Court!
Don't let them take it away!

* *(Alternate:)*
I love the Bill of Rights with all the
    fervor I possess,
And when I pray, I always say,
"Thank God for freedom of the press."

SEND THE MARINES

When someone makes a move
Of which we don't approve,
Who is it that always intervenes?
U.N. and O. A. S.,
They have their place, I guess,
But first send the Marines!

We'll send them all we've got,
John Wayne and Randolph Scott,
Remember those exciting fighting scenes?
To the shores of Tripoli,
But not to Mississippoli,

What do we do? We send the Marines!
For might makes right,

And till they've seen the light,
They've got to be protected,
All their rights respected,
Till somebody we like can be elected.

Members of the corps
All hate the thought of war,
They'd rather kill them off by peaceful means.
Stop calling it aggression,
We hate that expression.
We only want the world to know
That we support the status quo,
They love us ev'rywhere we go,
So when in doubt,
Send the Marines!

POLLUTION

1. If you visit American city,
    You will find it very pretty.
    Just two things of which you must beware:
    Don't drink the water and don't breathe the air.

    Pollution, Pollution,
    They got smog and sewage and mud,
    Turn on your tap and get hot and cold running
        crud.

2. See the halibuts and the sturgeons
    Being wiped out by detergeons.
    Fish gotta swim and birds gotta fly,
    But they don't last long if they try.

    Pollution, Pollution,
    You can use the latest toothpaste,
    And then rinse your mouth with industrial waste.

3. Just go out for a breath of air,
    And you'll be ready for Medicare,
    The city streets are really quite a thrill,
    If the hoods don't get you, the monoxide will.

    Pollution, Pollution,
    Wear a gas mask and a veil,
    Then you can breathe, long as you don't inhale.

4. Lots of things there that you can drink,
    But stay away from the kitchen sink,
    Throw out your breakfast garbage, and I've got a
        hunch
    That the folks downstream will drink it for lunch.

    So go to the city, see the crazy people there.
    Like lambs to the slaughter,
    They're drinking the water
    And breathing *(cough . . . .)* the air.

SO LONG, MOM
(A SONG FOR WORLD WAR III)

So long, Mom,
I'm off to drop the bomb,
So don't wait up for me,
But while you swelter
Down there in your shelter,
You can see me
On your T. V.

While we're attacking frontally,
Watch Brinkally and Huntally,
Describing contrapuntally
The cities we have lost.
No need for you to miss a minute of the
    agonizing holocaust.

Little Johnny Jones he was a U.S. pilot,
And no shrinking vi'let was he.
He was mighty proud when World War Three
                was declared,
He wasn't scared,
No siree!

And this is what he said on
His way to Armageddon:

So long, Mom,
I'm off to drop the bomb,

So don't wait up for me,
But though I may roam,
I'll come back to my home,
Although it may be
A pile of debris.

Remember, Mommy,
I'm off to get a commie,
So send me a salami,
And try to smile somehow.
I'll look for you when the war is over,
An hour and a half from now!

WHO'S NEXT?

First we got the bomb, and that was good,
'Cause we love peace and motherhood.
Then Russia got the bomb, but that's okay,
'Cause the balance of power's maintained that way.
    Who's next?

Then France got the bomb, but don't you grieve,
'Cause they're on our side (I believe).
China got the bomb, but have no fears,
'Cause they can't wipe us out for at least five years.
    Who's next?

Japan will have its own device,
Transistorized at half the price.
South Africa wants two, that's right:
One for the black and one for the white.
    Who's next?

Egypt's gonna get one too,
Just to use on you know who.
So Israel's getting tense,
Wants one in self defense.
"The Lord's our shepherd," says the psalm,
But just in case we better get a bomb.
    Who's next?

Luxembourg is next to go,
And (who knows?) maybe Monaco.
We'll try to stay serene and calm
When Alabama gets the bomb.
    Who's next?
Who's next?
Who's next?
Who's next?

I GOT IT FROM AGNES

I love my friends, and they love me,
We're just as close as we can be.
And just because we really care,
Whatever we get, we share!

1. I got it from Agnes,
    She got it from Jim.
    We all agree it must have been
    Louise who gave it to him.

    Now she got it from Harry,
    Who got it from Marie,
    And ev'rybody knows that Marie
    Got it from me.

2. Giles got it from Daphne,
    She got it from Joan,
    Who picked it up in County Cork,
    A-kissin' the Blarney Stone.

    Pierre gave it to Sheila,
    Who must have brought it there.
    He got it from François and Jacques,
    Aha, Lucky Pierre.

3. Max got it from Edith,
    Who gets it ev'ry spring.
    She got it from her Daddy,
    Who just gives her ev'rything.

She then gave it to Daniel,
Whose spaniel has it now.
Our dentist even got it,
And we're still wondering how.

4. But I got it from Agnes,
   Or maybe it was Sue,
   Or Millie or Billie or Gillie or Willie,
   It doesn' matter who.

It might have been at the pub,
or at the club, or in the loo,
And if you will be my friend,
then I might . . . (Mind you, I said "might") . . .
(*looks around audience, finally chooses someone,
grins, points to him or her and says:*)
Give it to you!

SILENT E

Who can turn a can into a cane?
Who can turn a pan into a pane?
It's not too hard to see,
It's Silent E.

Who can turn a cub into a cube?
Who can turn a tub into a tube?
It's elementary
For Silent E.

He took a pin and turned it into a pine.
He took a twin and turned him into twine.

Who can turn a cap into a cape?
Who can turn a tap into a tape?
A little glob becomes a globe instantly,
If you just add Silent E.

He turned a dam—Alikazam!—into a dame.
But my friend Sam stayed just the same.

Who can turn a man into a mane?
Who can turn a van into a vane?
A little hug becomes huge instantly.
Don't add W, Don't add X, And don't add Y or Z,
Just add Silent E.

L - Y

1. You're wearing your squeaky shoes,
   And right there taking a snooze
   Is a tiger, so how do you walk on by?
   (*loud whisper*)
   Silently, silently, Silent L.Y.

2. You're a secret agent man
   Who's after the secret plan.
   How do you act so they don't know you're a spy?
   (*acting suspiciously*)
   Normally, normally, Normal L. Y.

3. At an eating contest you boast
   That you can eat the most.
   How do you down your fiftieth piece of pie?
   (*nauseated*)
   Eagerly, eagerly, Eager L.Y.

4. On the lake your boat upset,
   And your clothes got soaking wet.
   How do you stand and wait for them to dry?
   (*shivering*)

D-d-d-d-d-d-patiently, D-d-d-d-d-d-patiently,
   D-d-d-d-d-d-patient L. Y.

5. In the public library
   You fall and hurt your knee.
   But the sign says QUIET PLEASE, so how can you
     cry?
   (*crying*)
   Quietly, quietly, Quiet L. Y.

6. As you walk along the street
   A porcupine you meet.
   How do you shake his hand when he says "hi"?
   (*warily*)
   Carefully, carefully, Careful L. Y.

7. You enter a very dark room,
   And sitting there in the gloom
   Is Dracula.
   Now how do you say goodbye?
   Immediately, immediately, Immediate L. Y.
   Bye bye!

THE VATICAN RAG

First you get down on your knees,
Fiddle with your rosaries,
Bow your head with great respect,
And genuflect, genuflect, genuflect!

Do whatever steps you want if
You have cleared them with the Pontiff,
Ev'rybody say his own
Kyrie eleison,
Doin' the Vatican Rag.

Get in line in that processional,
Step into that small confessional,
There the guy who's got religion'll
Tell you if your sin's original.
If it is, try playin' it safer,

Drink the wine and chew the wafer,
Two, four, six, eight,
Time to transubstantiate!

So get down upon your knees,
Fiddle with your rosaries,
Bow your head with great respect,
And genuflect, genuflect, genuflect!

Make a cross on your abdomen,
When in Rome do like a Roman,
Ave Maria,
Gee, it's good to see ya,
Gettin' ecstatic an' sorta dramatic an'
Doin' the Vatican
Rag!